GREEK AND ROMAN FASHIONS

Tom Tierney

DOVER PUBLICATIONS, INC.
Mineola, New York

Bibliographical Note

Greek and Roman Fashions is a new work, first published by Dover Publications, Inc., in 2001.

International Standard Book Number

ISBN-13: 978-0-486-41547-5
ISBN-10: 0-486-41547-3

Manufactured in the United States by Courier Corporation
41547303   2013
www.doverpublications.com

Introduction

I have presented ancient Greek and Roman fashions in one book because Roman fashions were adopted almost entirely from those of Greece. I also have included a few fashions of the pre-classic Greek and pre-Roman eras: from Phrygia, Mycenaea, the island of Crete, and the Etruscans of Italy. Our information about ancient Crete (ca. 2000–1500 B.C.) is limited to fragments of murals and some carvings and ceramics. Clothing designs were quite elegant and indicate skill in sewing and dressmaking, with pleating, set-in sleeves, layering, and embroidery used. The Cretans' imaginative jewelry shows great technical knowledge.

Among the people of Asia Minor who were precursors of classical Greek civilization were the Phrygians. Both sexes wore sewn garments with narrow, fitted sleeves and fitted leggings or hose (probably knitted). Garments often were delicately patterned (probably embroidered). Phrygian use of the draped scarf was ancestral to the classic Greek and Roman choice of garments that were draped, tied, and pinned.

Three items were basic to classic Greek dress: the *chiton* (pronounced *kite*-n), a linen shirtlike garment, the *peplos,* an overgarment worn only by women, and the *chlamys* (pronounced *klom*-iss), a cloak. These three garments were draped and girdled to create varied styles. Greek fashions from ca. 600 B.C. still showed many earlier influences, such as patterned fabrics and elaborately braided borders. By 500 B.C. the chiton was made of two long rectangles of fabric, of a width from elbow to elbow. The sides were stitched together for two-thirds of the length and the top opening was pinned to form two shoulder straps. Females often wore two *girdles,* or waistbands, with the fabric pouched over them. Men wore a single girdle at the waist. The chlamys now was a male garment. Women's cloaks (the *himation*), also rectangular, were much longer. Later, both sexes wore the himation over the chiton, and men wore it, with no other garment, for formal and state occasions. The common men and women usually wore only the short chiton.

North of what was to become Rome was the ancient country of Etruria. The Etruscan cloak, the *tabenna,* was semicircular. The Etruscans also wore a tunic similar to the Greek chiton. Etruscan women's robes, sewn with a fitted bodice and flared skirt, were worn with a short jacket or a cloak.

Probably early Roman dress for men was a shirtlike *tunica,* and a cloak, the *toga.* The toga, uniquely Roman, was similar in drape and use to the Greek chlamys, but semicircular and very long, with the width twice the length. (As Rome grew, so did the size of its togas.) The part of the toga that went over the left shoulder was pulled up and bloused in the front, forming a pocket called a *sinus.* Another type of Roman cloak, the *paenula,* was rather bell-shaped, sewn down the sides, and often worn with a hood. The tunica was sewn down both sides and usually had short sleeves. It was cut wide and girdled, much like the Greek chiton. To go outdoors dressed only in a tunica was considered bad form, except for workmen. A longer tunica *(tunica manicata)* did not become popular until about A.D. 300. Many men wore only the toga, apparently thinking that they appeared more "manly" in this single garment. On the tunica were worn badges of rank in the form of colored bands or braid, called *clavi.* For example, senators wore wide purple stripes called *laticlavia* and victorious generals wore golden embroidered palm-leaf stripes called *palmata.* The wearing of any kind of hose was forbidden by law in the city of Rome. However, as the empire waned, the military adopted breeches such as the Gauls and Persians wore—probably inspired by the chill of Britain and of desert nights.

The principal items of dress for Roman women were a shirt or chemise *(tunica intima),* a dress over it, and a cloaklike garment. The woman's tunica was similar in cut to the men's, but reached the floor. Often it was of light wool, but in later centuries sheer fabrics were used. Usually it was adorned at the shoulders with clasps or buttons. Most Roman women girdled the tunica under the breasts. Over this was worn a *stola,* cut exactly like the tunica, but with full sleeves. Its draping was considered an art form, and it often was adorned with colorful braids, pearls, and spangles. The third garment, the *palla,* was worn outside the house. At first the palla resembled the male toga, but later it became more voluminous and rectangular. On the street the women wore a veil called a *flammeum,* which was attached to the back of the hair and extended down the back.

Roman males usually pulled their togas over their heads when the weather was bad. Travelers sometimes wore hats of felt or braided straw. Laborers, sailors, and hunters often wore caps of leather or straw. At the height of the Roman Empire women's hairstyles became extremely elaborate and varied. Footwear was an important feature of Roman dress.

Women's shoe styles were similar to men's but were more elegantly decorated with gold braids, pearls, and jewels.

The abundant traces of color left on unearthed statuary show that ancient Greek costume was very colorful, as was Roman garb, but natural plant and mineral dyes produced softer tints than the synthetic dyes used now. Gold trims, jewels, and spangles decorated their fabrics, and beautifully made jewelry was worn.

The dates given in this book are not specific, because most of the fashions are based on artifacts that seldom can be dated exactly. In any case, styles did not change frequently.

Cretan nobility (ca. 2000–1200 B.C.)

The Cretan ideal was a slim-waisted figure for both men and women. Men usually wore only a decorated loincloth, and often women did too, but sometimes women wore corseted jackets to enhance their slim waists. The bosom was left bare. The corselets and tiered skirts show considerable skill in dressmaking. Bright, primary colors and earth tones were favored.

Mycenaean common folk (ca. 1500–1000 B.C.)

As in most civilizations, the common people wore a variation on the simple tunic. Archaeological fragments seem to indicate that the folk of Asia Minor (now often called the Mideast or the Middle East) decorated their tunics, which often were dyed in earth tones, with contrasting bands of fabric or embroidery.

Phrygian young woman and Amazon (ca. 1200–900 B.C.)

Most of the Greek mythology and legends with which we are familiar were Phrygian in origin—the story of King Midas, for example. The Phrygians excelled in metalwork, wood carving, sewing, knitting, and embroidery. The Phrygian cap became the symbol of liberated slaves in Rome, and, much later, the symbol of liberty during the French Revolution. Both women's sewn and girdled gowns, the Amazon's tights, and the other's cloak and cap are delicately embroidered.

The Greek *chiton* (ca. 500 B.C.)

The man's chiton, sometimes called a *camisa,* had one girdle or belt. The woman's usually had two. The bloused
area was called the *kolpus* (in the Roman adaptation it
was the *deploidion*). The basic Greek chiton was folded
down one side and open on the other. The back corners
were pinned to the front to form shoulder straps. Chitons
also could be floor length for both men and women.

The Greek *chlamys* (ca. 500 B.C.)

Basically a large rectangle of fabric, this standard men's cloak was draped over the left shoulder and pinned on the right. It could be worn over a chiton or alone. It was considered "manly" by youths and dandies to endure the elements in that single garment.

The Doric *peplos*

Originally worn in the province of Doris, this form of the chiton was one of the basic Greek women's garments. A huge rectangle of fabric was first folded across the top, then folded down one side, and pinned at the shoulders.

Just under the top flap it was girdled and bloused, and the draperies were carefully arranged. We get our modern word "peplum" from the fold in this garment.

The Ionic *chiton*

Another basic woman's garment, designed in the province of Ionia, this chiton was adopted throughout ancient Greece. It was an immense rectangle of fabric which was simply folded along one side and then pinned at intervals along the arms and at the shoulders. Girdled, it formed voluminous sleeves when carefully draped.

Fashionable Greek women (ca. 600–480 B.C.)

The woman on the left wears a variation on the Doric peplos; the other wears an arrangement of the Ionic chiton. Note the elaborate patterning (probably embroidery), as well as their intricate hairstyles. The woman on the left has her hair bound in a bandeau and her companion wears a coronet called a *stephanie* as well as a snoodlike affair to hold up her coiffure.

Greek statesman and high-ranking woman (ca. 540–500 B.C.)

He wears a cloak called a *himation,* which evolved from the chlamys but was both longer and wider. Both men and women wore the himation, but men usually wore it without other garments. It was considered rather formal attire. The woman wears a highly decorated version of the peplos.

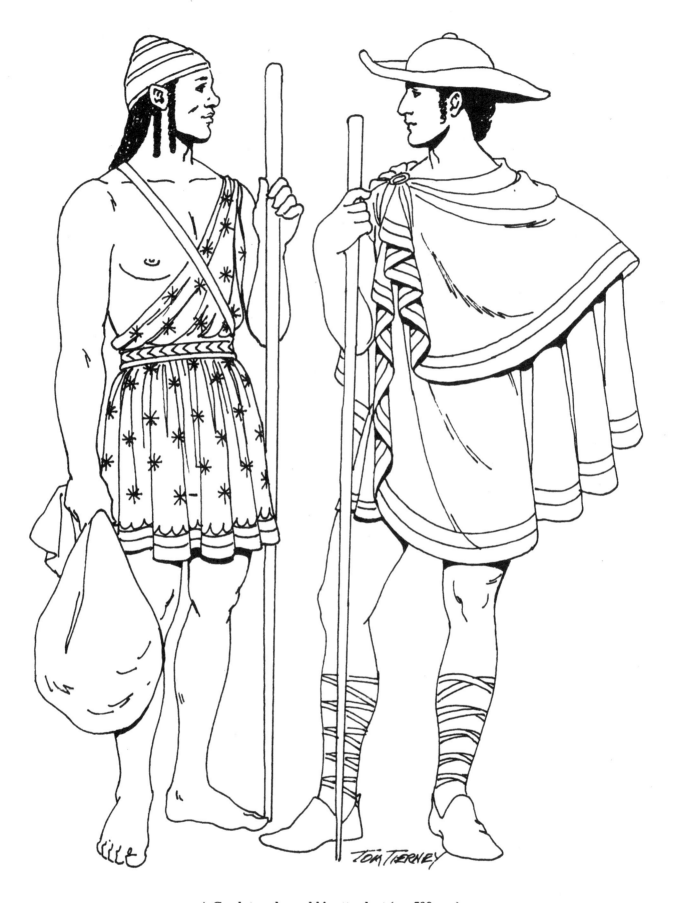

A Greek traveler and his attendant (ca. 500 B.C.)

The traveler wears a chlamys over a chiton, leather shoes laced to the midcalf, and a large-brimmed, bell-crowned sun hat of braided straw. The attendant wears a chiton, pinned over one shoulder only, with a leather *balteus* or chest band. His hat is a straw cap or *tatulus*.

Fashionable Greek women (ca. 500 B.C.)

The woman on the left wears a long tunica with a himation draped over the shoulder. On her head she wears a stephanie and on her wrists bracelets or armillas. The woman on the right wears a short chiton over a long one.

Both feature embroidered trims. She is wearing a decorative cloth cap plus a variation on the stephanie, and is holding some needlework.

11

Banquet guest and dancing girl (ca. 500 B.C.)

Most Greek banquets were strictly male affairs, with the attendees reclining on couches to dine, wearing only the himation and garlands of flowers in their hair. The guests usually were entertained by musicians and female dancers. This young woman wears a sheer, patterned himation draped over one shoulder and falling in a train at the back.

Greek rustic couple (ca. 480 B.C.)

The girl wears an Ionic chiton, girdled and shortened, over a long, short-sleeved chiton. They are both of lightweight linen, which has been twisted while damp to form broomstick pleats. Her knit cap is held in place by a stephanie. The boy wears a short, broomstick-pleated chiton under a short chlamys with a sun hat hanging in back.

Dancing girl and banquet guest (ca. 470–450 B.C.)

This sensuous dancer is wearing a sheer version of the Doric peplos. The banquet guest admiring her perform- ance is wearing a himation decorated with a wide band. In his hair he wears a garland of laurel leaves.

Greek warriors (ca. 440 B.C.)

The Greek warrior on the left wears a soft linen chiton under his metal breastplate and short metal (chain-mail) skirt. His metal helmet with neck shield sports a plume of red horsehair, and he wears metal shin armor. The foot soldier of lower rank wears a short tunic with an overskirt in brightly colored linen. His metal helmet has a less impressive plume than his superior's.

15

Greek woman and her maidservant (ca. 450 B.C.)

The woman wears a variation of the Ionic chiton, with a sheer himation folded and draped to simulate an off-the-shoulder flounce and a peplos. Her cloth cap is trimmed with ribbon. Her maid wears a wide-sleeved, girdled chiton over a long chiton. Her hair is bound with ribbon. Chitons often were layered, one over the other, to achieve various draping effects as well as color combinations.

Greek women (ca. 440–190 B.C.)

Both of these young women wear a peplos and a chiton with two different styles of shoulder girdles. The wearing of the girdle wrapped around the shoulder and crossed in the back or front was originally a male style, but as Greek women's dress evolved, they adopted it.

Greek guard or policeman and a young woman (ca. 400 B.C.)

He is wearing a metal helmet with a broad brim and a thigh-length chiton of brightly colored linen with boldly patterned geometric borders. She is wearing a chiton with a himation around her shoulders.

Greek couple dressed for travel (ca. 300 B.C.)

The woman wears a bordered himation draped over her head, atop which is a small straw sun hat called a *tholia*. She carries a braided-straw fan shaped like a leaf. The man wears a himation over a long tunic and has on a straw sun hat with a bell crown, the *petasos*.

19

Greek farmer and shepherd (ca. 300 B.C.)

The farmer wears a coarse cloth skullcap over his short-cropped hair. In ancient times men wore their hair long, but during the Persian wars (5th century B.C.) it became the mode to cut it short. His tunic is of coarse linen or wool and his legs are protected by soft leather guards bound with leather thongs. The shepherd wears a wide-brimmed straw hat, a coarse leather cape, a sheered-sheepskin tunic, and leather boots. Rural men and urban laborers dressed like these men throughout most of Greek and Roman history.

Serving girl and Greek matron (ca. 250 B.C.)

The serving girl is wearing a long chiton with a single girdle. On her head she wears a cloth cap. Her mistress's garb is a patterned Ionic chiton with a himation over the shoulder, girdled at the waist. Note the elaborate embroidered band on the edge of the himation and the weight on its corner. The weight enhanced the line of the drape.

Etruscan couple (ca. 1000 B.C.)

The Etruscans probably were the ancestors of Rome's founders. In any case, they greatly influenced the Romans' early dress. The Etruscan women wore sewn dresses, which either had a fitted peplos or a sewn jacket (it is dif-ficult to be sure from the surviving depictions of their garments). The men seem to have worn a fitted long tunic with a cloak called a *tabenna*. Both men's and women's garments were decorated with broad stripes of color.

Etruscan couple (ca. 750 B.C.)

The woman's dress is belted and has a capelet, which is pinned at the shoulder. The man is wearing a tabenna, semicircular in cut, draped over his shoulders. The Etruscan men allowed their long hair to hang over their shoulders, sometimes braiding it in the back.

Etruscan dancers (ca. 500 B.C.)

The female dancer wears a sewn, fitted gown with flared skirt and set-in wide sleeves. The sleeves and skirt are fringed. The dress is edged in a geometric-patterned band and the fabric is patterned, probably with embroidery. Her conical hat is a *tutulus* and her hair is worn in long, hanging twists in the front and falls freely in back. Her shoes could have been soft leather or felt. Her partner wears a tabenna (cloak) with a band of bright color and soft leather slippers with pointed toes. He wears a bandeau of laurel leaves in his hair.

Roman patricians (ca. 750 B.C.)

These men are wearing the banded toga. It is seen here in one of its simplest drapes. Note the curve of its banded edge. The weight on the two bottom corners of each toga enables the graceful wave effect to remain in place.

Roman workers (ca. 750–300 B.C.)

The worker on the left wears the simplest of chitons, which is short, girdled at the waist, and draped over one shoulder. His partner wears a short tunica, girdled at the waist. It is closed over the shoulders and has short sleeves.

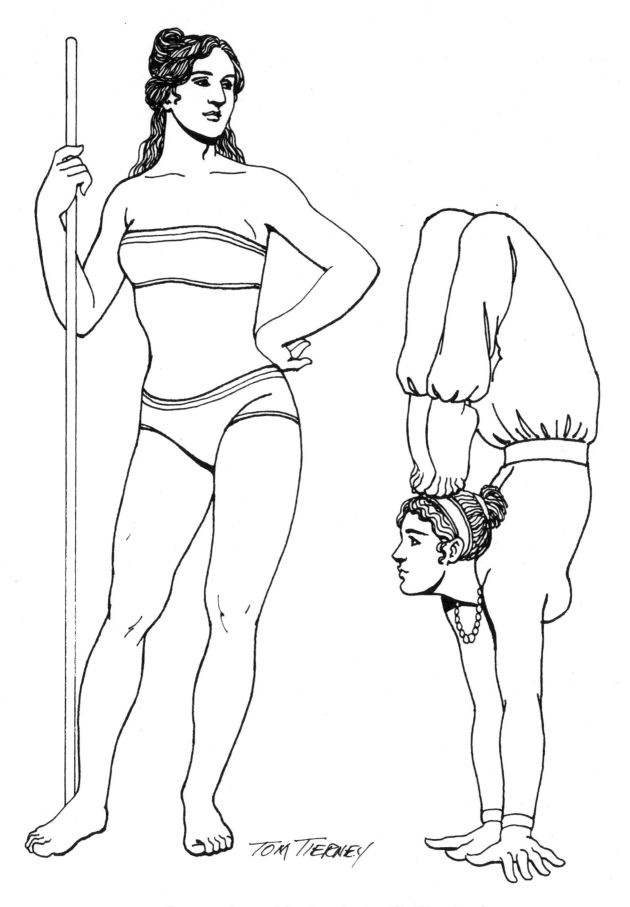

Roman gymnast and Greek acrobat (ca. 450–300 B.C.)

The gymnast, on the left, is wearing a *zona* (the term refers to the combination of knit brassiere and briefs seen here). The acrobat wears a knit top and Persian-style pantaloons.

Roman gladiator and his Greek servant (ca. 300 B.C.)

The gladiator wears an asymmetrically draped tunic with the back skirt pulled between the legs and tucked into the wide leather belt in front to form shorts. One arm and shoulder are protected with padded and studded leather, and he wears ankle boots. He is holding a shield and a chain mace. His servant wears two rectangles of fabric pinned at the shoulders, and a band on his hair.

Religious pilgrims (ca. 150 B.C.)

The man wears a long, bordered toga over a short-sleeved long tunica. (For religious ceremonies the toga was worn covering the head.) Over a long tunica, the woman is wearing the *palla,* which differed from the semicircular toga by being rectangular in shape. Over her head she wears a veil (a *flammeum*—later called a *ricinium*).

Germanic mercenary foot soldier and Roman horseman (ca. A.D. 100–250)

The foot soldier wears a leather-fringed loincloth and decorated belts around his waist. Over his shoulders he wears a *paenula* with a hood *(focalia)*. He is carrying a shield and a javelin, and wears a sword and a dagger. The horseman wears a simple tunica with a fitted shoulder cape, over knitted breeches. He has a metal helmet, a horseman's spear, a long sword *(spatha)*, and a tooled and painted leather shield.

Roman senator and woman (ca. 100–25 B.C.)

The Roman statesman wears the classic toga over a long tunica. His companion wears an Ionic chiton of a sheer fabric with a palla draped about her hips and over her arm. Her compact hairdo is crowned by a simple stephanie. Both wear leather sandals; his are partly enclosed.

31

A farm couple (ca. 50–25 B.C.)

These rural folk are dressed for travel to the marketplace in the city. The man wears a short tunic, full enough to form three-quarter-length sleeves by girdling it. His outer garment is the paenula. His ankles are wrapped with bands of cloth above his sandals. The woman wears a Doric chiton-style gown with a himation draped over the head and about the body.

Roman captain *(centurion)* and high officer (ca. A.D. 150–200)

The centurion wears metal scale armor over his pleated tunic, and metal greaves or shin armor *(ocrae)*. Over the scale armor he wears silver decorations of merit, suspended from ribbons. A mantle is draped over his left shoulder and arm. He carries a vinewood stick (the mark of a centurion) and his helmet, with the crest placed sideways. The officer wears leather armor and a leather skirt over a cloth tunic and knitted breeches. His mantle is of red-purple wool, and his helmet bears a "caterpillar" style of crest. His shield is in the round "Greek style."

Roman soldier and traveler (ca. A.D. 150)

The soldier wears a metal helmet with a single red plume, a short, circular cloak over leather armor, a short undertunic, and knit breeches. His short sword hangs from a tooled leather bandoleer. The traveler wears a paenula with a hood called *cucullus*. The paenula eventually replaced the toga. Below his knit breeches he wears *fascia* or *tibialie,* wrappings of cloth (adopted from the Gauls), to keep the lower leg warm.

Gladiators and attendant (ca. A.D. 250–300)

The attendant wears an unbelted tunica with a band of a contrasting color down the center. He is blowing a horn (the *cornu*) to announce the next contest. The net fighter in the center (a *retiarius*) wears only a belt and loincloth, leather greaves (shin guards), a metal shoulder plate, and a chain-mail sleeve and glove. He carries a metal net and *trident* spear. The Thracian gladiator on the right carries a *gladius* (sword) and a shield. He wears a belted loincloth. His visored helmet, shoulder and arm protectors, and greaves all are of metal.

Coach and Gallic gladiator (ca. A.D. 250–300)

The coach holds his hand up as he gives instructions. He wears a wide, girdled tunic with colored laticlavia (stripes) from shoulder to hem, and carries an official's rod. The gladiator is dressed in the Gallic style, with a broadbrimmed, visored metal helmet. He wears a loincloth with a wide leather belt, and leather bandoleers and shoulder straps. His sword arm is bound with leather. He wears a leather-and-metal leg shield on one leg, a leather ankle guard on the other, and carries a leather shield.

Man and woman in everyday garb (ca. A.D. 25)

The man wears a short tunica or *cyclas* with long, fitted sleeves, and a short cloak. He wears high leather boots.

The woman wears a tunica and a palla. These fashions would remain popular until about A.D. 200.

Variations on the *toga praetexta* (ca. A.D. 150–200)

The toga remained the formal wear for statesmen and philosophers.
The term "praetexta" applied when the toga had a purple border.

Roman bride and attendant (ca. 25 B.C.–A.D. 300)

During the imperial period the Roman bride wore a saffron-yellow veil (flammeum or ricinium). Under the veil were three stuffed pads to add height. Her gown was usually an asymmetrically draped tunica under a palla. She carries a soft leather fan. The attendant wears only a palla, supported by a bandoleer across the shoulder. Large jewelry was favored.

High-ranking women of the imperial period (ca. 25 B.C.–A.D. 300)

Variations on the draping of the tunica and the palla were seemingly endless, and the color combinations were highly creative, ranging from pastels to full chroma. Roman styles of hairdressing became more and more elaborate during the imperial period. The woman on the right holds a peacock feather, suitable for use as a light fan.

A Roman senator and his family (ca. A.D. 300–487)

The woman wears a tunica with a band of a contrasting color down the front, under a palla draped over her shoulders. Her hair is elaborately curled and braided.

The child is dressed in a toga like his father's, but not banded. By this time the toga is narrower and much longer, allowing for more complex draping.

Grecian hairstyles and headgear (ca. 750–300 B.C.)

The sequence shows changes progressing from
the ancient Archaic period to the Hellenic.

Roman hairstyles and headgear (ca. 300–100 B.C.)
A variety of hairpins and clasps are shown.

VESTAL VIRGIN

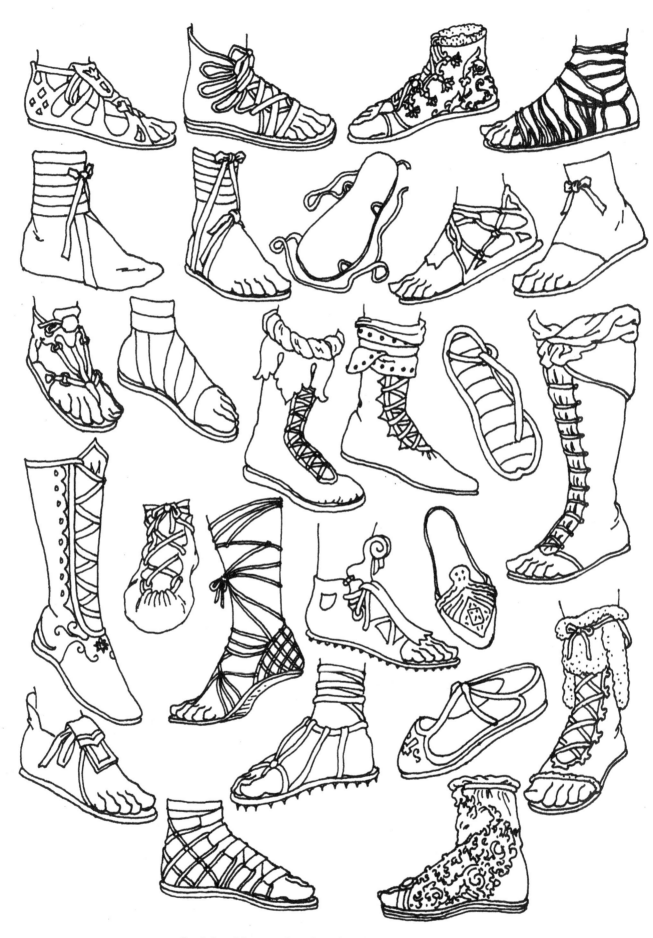

Sandal and boot styles of ancient Greece and Rome